Cello Time Runners

Cello accompaniment book

Kathy and David Blackwell

Teacher's note
These duet parts are written to accompany the tunes in *Cello Time Runners*. They are an alternative to the piano accompaniments or audio tracks, and are not designed to be used with those items.

We are grateful to Alison Ingram and Claire Saddler for all their help in road-testing these duets.

Kathy and David Blackwell

OXFORD
UNIVERSITY PRESS

OXFORD
UNIVERSITY PRESS
Great Clarendon Street, Oxford OX2 6DP,
United Kingdom

Oxford University Press is a department of the University of Oxford.
It furthers the University's objective of excellence in research, scholarship,
and education by publishing worldwide. Oxford is a registered trade mark of
Oxford University Press in the UK and in certain other countries

This collection Oxford University Press 2002, 2014, and 2023.

Impression: 1

ISBN 978-019-356607-1

Cover illustration by Martin Remphry

Music and text origination Julia Bovee
Printed in Great Britain

Contents

1. Start the show

(for Clare)

KB & DB

2. Banyan tree

Jamaican folk tune

3. Heat haze

KB & DB

4. Medieval tale

KB & DB

5. Chase in the dark

KB & DB

With menace

6. Spy movie

Creepily

KB & DB

7. Romani band

KB & DB

With energy

8. Busy day

9. On the go!

KB & DB

Lively

10. That's how it goes!: page 14
11. Blue whale: page 15

12. Mean street chase

KB & DB

10. That's how it goes!

KB & DB

11. Blue whale

Gently

KB & DB

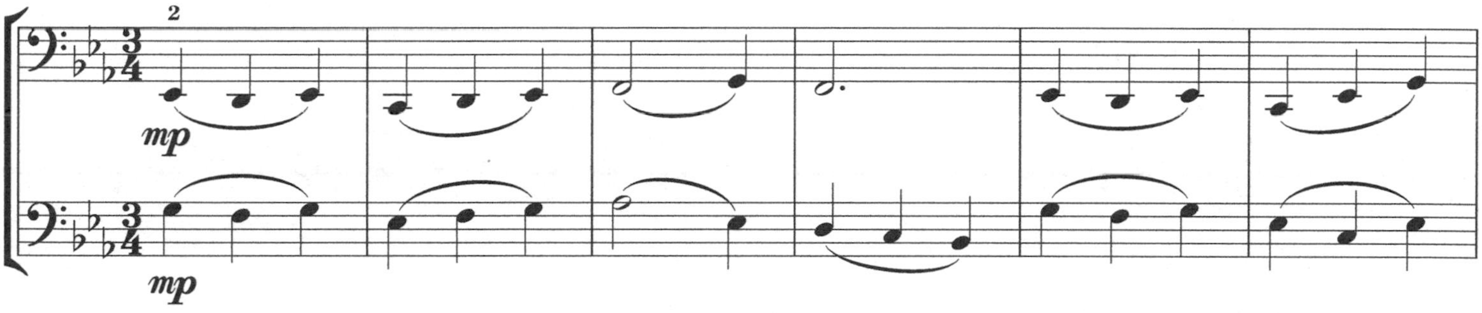

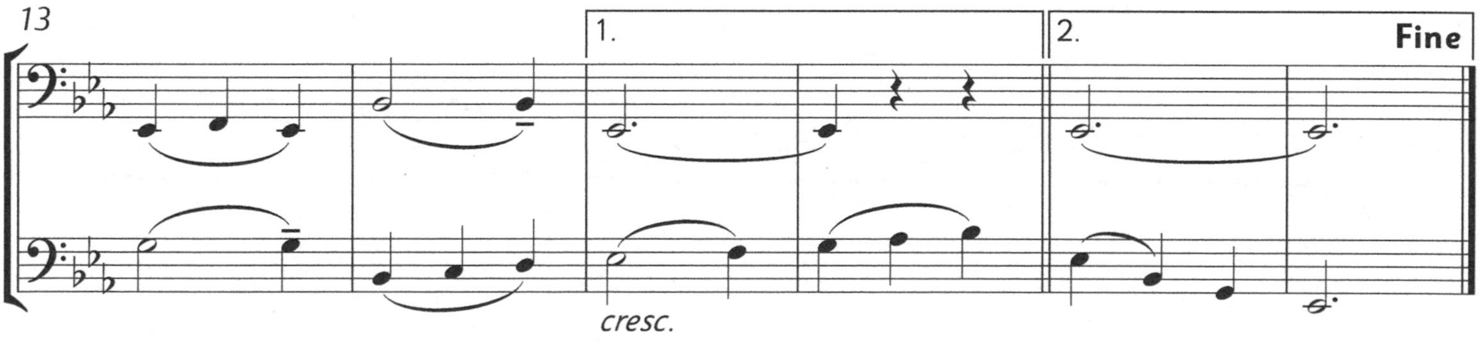

13. Allegretto

Allegretto

Mozart

14. Cornish May song

Cornish folk tune

Lively

15. Noël

Daquin

Allegretto

16. Prelude from 'Te Deum'

Maestoso

Charpentier

17. Paris café

KB & DB

18. Starry night

KB & DB

7
13
mf
mf
19
poco rit.
dim.
dim.
a tempo
25
mp
mp
31
rall.
dim.
dim.
p
p

19. Cello Time rag

KB & DB

17
f
mf
21
mp
mp
25
29
mf
mf
33
cresc.
f
cresc.
f

20. Caribbean sunshine

Calypso

KB & DB

21. Jacob's dance

KB & DB

22. Song from the show: page 30

23. The road to Donegal

KB & DB

Can also be bowed (♩ ♪ ♩ ♪) etc.

24. Cat's eyes

With menace (Swing)

KB & DB

21
arco
25
arco
29
pizz.
33
pizz.
37
arco
(pizz.)

22. Song from the show

KB & DB

25. Mexican fiesta

KB & DB

26. Summer evening

Flowing

KB & DB

27. Extension rock

KB & DB

28. Show off!

Funky

KB & DB

29. You and me

KB & DB

Happy

30. One day

Simply
KB & DB
mp espress.
mp espress.
mf
mf
dim.
dim.
mp
mp
Fine
mp
mp
mf
mf
dim.
dim.
D.C. al Fine

31. Aerobics

KB & DB

32. Hungarian folk dance

Lively

KB & DB

22
X4
1
27
f
f
32
37
2nd time accelerando
mf (ff)
p
mf (ff)
sim.
42
1.
2.
ff
ff

33. Show stopper

KB & DB

Strongly

23
ff
ff
27
f
ff
f
cresc.
ff
31
mf
mp
mf
mp
35
cresc.
cresc.
39
mf
cresc.
f
ff
mf
cresc.
f
ff

34. Farewell to Skye

(for Iain)

Peaceful

KB & DB